Chords Rule!

Seven Later Elementary Level Piano Solos
Based on Block and Broken Chords
by

Carolyn Miller

Contents

12193

The Parade

Moderato

Carolyn Miller

12193

1 2 5
mf
1 2 5
L.H.
f
L.H.
R.H.

Ripples in the Water

Moderato; flowing

Carolyn Miller

mf
poco rit.
D.C. al Coda
Coda
8va
R.H.
L.H.
pp
8vb

Processional

Like a march

Carolyn Miller

5
4
1 2 3 1
R.H.

Sailing in the Wind

Carolyn Miller

Moderato *On repeat play both hands one octave lover.*

p
mp
mf
f
rit.
L.H.
D.C. al Coda
Coda
f
mf
mp
poco rit.
8vb

Polynesian Sunset

Gently

Carolyn Miller

mf
D.S. al Coda
Coda
molto ritard.
pp

Get It Together

Carolyn Miller

Rhythmic

8vb

Mt. Everest

Moderato

Carolyn Miller

L.H.
L.H.
L.H.
mf
L.H.
L.H.
L.H.
L.H.
f
L.H.

8va
8va
ff